Author biography

Yuvraj Singh, at the age of 19, is a passionate and dedicated individual committed to empowering students and young adults in their journey through higher education. Born with a love for learning and a natural curiosity about the world, Yuvraj embarked on his own college adventure with a strong desire to make a positive impact on the lives of his peers.

Hailing from a diverse background, Yuvraj has experienced firsthand the joys and challenges of student life. His personal encounters with academic pressures, relationship dynamics, and career uncertainties have fueled his determination to share his knowledge and experiences to support and inspire others.

Driven by a deep belief in the transformative power of education, Yuvraj has honed his writing skills and research acumen to provide practical guidance and valuable insights to fellow students. His ability to distill complex concepts into relatable and accessible information has garnered him recognition as a trusted voice in the realm of student life.

Yuvraj's passion for personal development and mental well-being led him to explore various disciplines, including psychology, mindfulness, and self-care practices. His dedication to nurturing his own emotional resilience and fostering healthy relationships has equipped him with a wealth of knowledge and strategies that he shares generously in his writing.

With an entrepreneurial spirit and a keen eye for opportunity, Yuvraj has also sought practical experiences beyond the classroom. He has actively engaged in part-time jobs and internships, allowing him to gain firsthand insights into the professional world and the challenges faced by young adults entering the workforce.

Yuvraj's commitment to empowering students extends beyond his writing. He actively volunteers his time in mentorship programs, offering guidance and support to his peers. Through workshops and speaking engagements, he has inspired countless individuals to embrace personal growth, navigate challenges with resilience, and create a well-rounded student experience.

In addition to his dedication to student empowerment, Yuvraj is an avid reader, an aspiring musician, and a lover of outdoor adventures. When he's not immersed in the world of academia or writing, you can find him exploring nature, strumming his guitar, or delving into thought-provoking books that expand his horizons.

As a young author, Yuvraj aspires to make a lasting impact on the lives of students around the world. Through his writing, he aims to empower individuals to embrace change, cultivate resilience, and thrive in their pursuit of knowledge and personal growth.

The Realities of Student Life Navigating Challenges and Embracing Growth

Navigating Challenges and Embracing Growth in the Journey of Higher Education

Yuvraj Singh

ISBN 978-93-5667-980-1
© Yuvraj Singh 2023

Published in India 2023 by Pencil

A brand of
One Point Six Technologies Pvt. Ltd.
Unit no. 26, Ground Floor, Building A1,
Wadala Truck Terminal Road,
Near Post Office, Antop Hill, Mumbai - 400037
E connect@thepencilapp.com
W www.thepencilapp.com

DISCLAIMER: *The opinions expressed in this book are those of the authors and do not purport to reflect the views of the Publisher.*

With "Thriving Through Student Life: Navigating Challenges and Embracing Growth," Yuvraj Singh shares his passion, knowledge, and personal experiences to inspire and guide students through the transformative journey of higher education.

CONTENTS

Introduction

Welcome to "Thriving Through Student Life: Navigating Challenges and Embracing Growth." This book is your comprehensive guide to making the most of your college years, equipping you with valuable insights, practical strategies, and empowering advice to navigate the diverse aspects of student life successfully.

The journey through higher education is a transformative time filled with excitement, self-discovery, and new opportunities. It is also a period that comes with its fair share of challenges and uncertainties. From academic pressures to personal growth, from relationships to career planning, every aspect of student life plays a significant role in shaping your future.

In this book, we have curated a collection of chapters that address the key areas of concern for students like yourself. Each chapter is designed to provide you with comprehensive information, actionable steps, and real-life examples to guide you on your path to success and fulfillment.

We begin by exploring the fundamental skills required for academic excellence. From effective study techniques to time management strategies, you will learn how to maximize your learning potential and achieve your academic goals.

Next, we delve into the realm of personal development. Understanding oneself, managing emotions, and nurturing mental well-being are essential components of a thriving student life. We equip you with the tools and insights necessary to navigate stress, build resilience, and prioritize self-care.

Building meaningful relationships and fostering a sense of community is another crucial aspect of the college experience. In chapters dedicated to relationships and social interactions, we guide you in developing healthy friendships, navigating romantic partnerships; and setting boundaries that foster respect and growth.

As you progress through your college years, thoughts of the future and career aspirations may loom large. Fear not! We dedicate chapters to career exploration, financial management, and gaining practical experience through internships and part-time jobs. You will gain valuable insights into industry trends, financial planning, and strategies for building a strong foundation for your professional journey.

Throughout this book, we emphasize the importance of embracing change, adapting to new situations, and seeking opportunities for personal growth. We provide you with the necessary tools to overcome challenges, make informed decisions, and thrive in the ever-evolving landscape of student life.

Whether you are just beginning your college adventure or are already immersed in the experience, "Thriving Through Student Life" serves as your trusted companion, offering guidance and support every step of the way. The knowledge and skills imparted within these pages will empower you to embrace the opportunities that college life presents and create a meaningful and successful journey towards your future aspirations.

Remember, you have the potential to not only survive but thrive through student life. Let this book be your roadmap to unlocking your full potential and making the most of this transformative chapter in your life.

So, get ready to embark on a journey of growth, self-discovery, and achievement. Together, let's navigate the challenges, seize the opportunities, and build a foundation for a bright and fulfilling future.

The Transition; From High School to College

In this chapter, we delve into the significant transition from high school to college and provide insights, guidance, and practical strategies to navigate this period of change successfully. We understand that this transition can be both exciting and challenging, as you leave behind familiar routines and enter a new academic and social environment.We begin by discussing the differences between high school and college, highlighting the key changes that students typically encounter. We address the academic expectations, classroom dynamics, and the increased level of independence and responsibility that come with college life. By understanding and acknowledging these differences, you can better prepare yourself for the transition ahead.Next, we provide strategies for managing the academic aspects of the transition. We discuss the importance of developing effective study habits, time management skills, and organizational strategies to meet the demands of college coursework. We offer advice on setting realistic goals, seeking academic support when needed, and utilizing resources available on campus to enhance your learning experience.Within this chapter, we also explore the social and personal aspects of the transition. We address topics such as making new friends, adjusting to a diverse student body, and managing homesickness or feelings of loneliness. We provide tips on building a support system, getting involved in campus activities, and embracing new experiences to foster a sense of belonging and connection.Furthermore, we discuss the emotional aspects of the transition. We acknowledge that leaving behind familiar environments and entering into a new phase of life can bring about a range of emotions. We offer strategies for managing stress, homesickness, and the pressures of transitioning to college. We emphasize the importance of self-care, seeking support from friends and family, and utilizing campus resources such as counseling services to navigate these emotional challenges.Additionally, we explore the practical considerations of the transition, including financial aspects, living arrangements, and adapting to a new routine. We provide guidance on budgeting, managing expenses, and understanding financial aid options. We also offer tips on navigating dorm life, establishing a healthy work-life balance, and developing self-discipline and time-management skills.Throughout this chapter, we incorporate real-life stories and experiences of students who have successfully transitioned from high school to college. Their stories serve as inspiration and provide relatable examples of the challenges and triumphs that come with this transition.By the end of this chapter, you will have gained valuable insights and practical strategies to navigate the transition from high school to college with confidence and resilience. You will be equipped to manage the academic, social, emotional, and practical aspects of this significant life change, ensuring a smoother and more fulfilling transition into your college experience.Remember, the transition from high school to college is a time of growth, self-discovery, and new opportunities. By embracing this transition and utilizing the tools and knowledge provided in this chapter, you can navigate the challenges and embrace the exciting possibilities that await you in your college journey.

Finding Your Tribe; Building a Supportive Network

In this chapter, we explore the importance of finding your tribe and building a supportive network during your college journey. We understand that the connections you form and the support system you create can greatly impact your overall well-being, personal growth, and success.We begin by discussing the concept of a "tribe" or a community of like-minded individuals who share similar interests, values, and goals. We emphasize the significance of finding your tribe as a means of finding a sense of belonging and support during your college years. Whether it's a group of friends, classmates, or individuals with shared hobbies or passions, your tribe can provide a sense of camaraderie, encouragement, and a safe space for self-expression.Next, we delve into the various ways to find your tribe on campus. We discuss student organizations, clubs, and extracurricular activities that align with your interests and provide opportunities for connection. We highlight the importance of stepping out of your comfort zone, attending events, and actively engaging in activities to meet new people and expand your social network.Within this chapter, we also address the qualities of a supportive network. We discuss the importance of surrounding yourself with individuals who uplift and inspire you, who share your values and goals, and who provide emotional support during both challenging and joyful times. We provide guidance on identifying and nurturing healthy friendships and relationships that contribute positively to your personal growth.Furthermore, we explore the benefits of a supportive network in various aspects of student life. We discuss how a strong support system can help you navigate academic challenges, provide motivation and accountability, and offer valuable insights and resources. We also delve into the emotional support that comes from having a supportive network, including stress relief, encouragement, and a sense of belonging.Additionally, we address the reciprocal nature of building a supportive network. We discuss the importance of being an active and supportive member of your tribe, offering your own strengths, skills, and support to others. We emphasize the value of fostering a community built on mutual respect, empathy, and collaboration.Throughout this chapter, we incorporate real-life examples and stories of students who have found their tribes and experienced the transformative power of a supportive network. Their experiences highlight the positive impact of community-building and provide inspiration for your own journey.By the end of this chapter, you will have gained a deeper understanding of the importance of finding your tribe and building a supportive network during your college years. You will have acquired strategies for connecting with like-minded individuals, nurturing healthy relationships, and actively participating in a community that fosters personal growth and support.Remember, finding your tribe goes beyond simply making friends—it's about cultivating a community that uplifts, supports, and encourages you to be your authentic self. Building a supportive network will not only enhance your college experience but also contribute to your overall well-being and success. So, embark on the journey of finding your tribe and watch as your connections empower you to thrive in all areas of student life.

Academic Demands; Balancing Workload and Time Management

In this chapter, we delve into the academic demands that students face in higher education and provide practical strategies for balancing workload and mastering time management. We understand that navigating coursework, assignments, exams, and deadlines can be overwhelming, and effective time management is crucial for academic success.We begin by addressing the common challenges students encounter when it comes to managing their academic workload. From heavy course loads to multiple assignments and competing priorities, we shed light on the realities of academic demands. We emphasize the importance of developing a proactive and organized approach to tackle these challenges head-on.Next, we provide strategies for effective time management. We discuss the significance of creating a realistic schedule, prioritizing tasks, and breaking them down into manageable chunks. We offer tips on setting goals, utilizing productivity tools and techniques, and overcoming procrastination. By implementing these strategies, you can optimize your time, increase productivity, and reduce stress associated with academic workload.Within this chapter, we also explore techniques for efficient studying and learning. We discuss effective note-taking methods, active reading strategies, and optimizing study environments. We delve into the benefits of creating study plans, utilizing resources such as libraries and study groups, and seeking clarification from professors or teaching assistants when needed. By employing these techniques, you can enhance your learning experience and retain information more effectively.Furthermore, we address the importance of self-care and maintaining a healthy work-life balance. We emphasize that effective time management goes beyond academic tasks and extends to personal well-being. We discuss the significance of taking breaks, engaging in hobbies and recreational activities, and ensuring adequate rest and sleep. By prioritizing self-care, you can rejuvenate your mind and body, improving focus and overall academic performance.Additionally, we explore the resources available on campus to support academic success. We discuss the importance of utilizing academic support services, such as tutoring centers, writing labs, and academic advisors. We highlight the benefits of seeking assistance when facing challenges or needing additional guidance. These resources can provide valuable insights, feedback, and support tailored to your academic needs.Throughout this chapter, we incorporate practical examples, success stories, and tips from students who have mastered the art of balancing workload and time management. Their experiences serve as inspiration and offer relatable guidance to help you overcome academic hurdles and excel in your studies.By the end of this chapter, you will have gained a deeper understanding of the academic demands of higher education and acquired effective strategies for balancing workload and managing your time. You will be equipped with practical tools and techniques to optimize your study habits, increase productivity, and achieve academic success while maintaining a healthy work-life balance.Remember, academic demands are a significant aspect of student life, but with the right mindset, skills, and strategies, you can confidently navigate your coursework and achieve your academic goals. Embrace the principles outlined in this chapter, and watch as you develop the ability to excel academically while maintaining a fulfilling and balanced student life.

Financial Pressures; Budgeting and Financial Independence

In this chapter, we explore the financial pressures that students often face during their college years and provide insights, tips, and strategies for effective budgeting and achieving financial independence. We understand that managing finances can be a significant source of stress, and having a solid grasp of budgeting and financial independence is essential for a successful college experience.We begin by addressing the common financial challenges students encounter, such as tuition fees, textbooks, housing costs, and daily expenses. We discuss the importance of understanding your financial situation and creating a realistic budget that aligns with your income and expenses. By gaining a clear picture of your financial standing, you can make informed decisions and develop strategies to achieve your financial goals.Next, we delve into the concept of budgeting and its significance in managing your finances. We provide practical tips for creating a budget, tracking expenses, and setting financial priorities. We emphasize the importance of distinguishing between needs and wants, making conscious spending choices, and identifying areas where you can cut back or save money. By implementing effective budgeting practices, you can gain control over your finances and alleviate financial stress.Within this chapter, we also discuss the importance of financial independence and exploring opportunities to generate income while studying. We explore part-time job options, internships, and work-study programs that can provide financial support and valuable professional experience. We offer advice on balancing work and academics, managing time effectively, and leveraging these opportunities to enhance your skills and future career prospects.Furthermore, we address the importance of financial literacy and knowledge about financial resources available to students. We discuss the significance of understanding banking, credit cards, loans, and financial aid options. We provide guidance on researching scholarships, grants, and other forms of financial assistance. By being proactive in seeking financial support, you can alleviate some of the financial pressures associated with student life.Additionally, we explore strategies for saving money and making smart financial decisions. We discuss the benefits of comparison shopping, utilizing student discounts, and practicing frugality without compromising on essential needs. We also emphasize the importance of building an emergency fund and planning for future expenses, such as post-graduation plans or repayment of student loans.Throughout this chapter, we incorporate real-life examples, success stories, and practical advice from students who have successfully managed their finances during their college years. Their experiences offer insights into effective financial management and provide inspiration for your own financial journey.By the end of this chapter, you will have gained a deeper understanding of the financial pressures faced by students and acquired practical strategies for budgeting and achieving financial independence. You will be equipped with the knowledge and tools to make informed financial decisions, manage your expenses effectively, and work towards financial stability and success throughout your college journey and beyond.Remember, by adopting responsible financial habits and being proactive in managing your finances, you can navigate the financial pressures of student life with confidence and set a strong foundation for your future financial well-being.

Mental Health Matters; Coping with Stress and Anxiety

In this chapter, we delve into the crucial topic of mental health and focus specifically on coping with stress and anxiety, which are common challenges faced by many students. We recognize that the demands of student life can be overwhelming, and prioritizing mental well-being is essential for a fulfilling and successful college experience.We begin by acknowledging the prevalence of stress and anxiety among students and their impact on academic performance, relationships, and overall well-being. We emphasize the importance of understanding the signs and symptoms of stress and anxiety, as well as the need to prioritize mental health as an integral part of student life.Next, we explore various coping mechanisms and strategies for managing stress effectively. We discuss the significance of self-care practices, such as maintaining a healthy lifestyle, getting regular exercise, practicing mindfulness, and engaging in relaxation techniques. We also emphasize the importance of seeking support from friends, family, and mental health professionals when needed, as reaching out for help is a sign of strength and resilience.Within this chapter, we provide insights into developing resilience and cultivating a positive mindset. We discuss strategies for reframing negative thoughts, managing perfectionism, and setting realistic expectations. We explore the power of self-compassion and the importance of practicing self-care, self-acceptance, and self-reflection. By developing these skills, you can navigate the challenges of student life with greater resilience and emotional well-being.Furthermore, we address the role of time management and work-life balance in managing stress and anxiety. We provide practical tips for prioritizing tasks, setting boundaries, and creating a schedule that allows for adequate rest and relaxation. We explore the benefits of engaging in activities that bring joy and fulfillment, such as hobbies, socializing, and pursuing personal interests outside of academics.Additionally, we discuss the importance of fostering a supportive and understanding campus environment for mental health. We address the resources available on campus, such as counseling services, support groups, and mental health initiatives. We encourage students to take advantage of these resources and to actively participate in creating a culture that promotes mental well-being and reduces the stigma surrounding mental health issues.Throughout this chapter, we incorporate personal stories, testimonials, and practical advice from students who have navigated their own experiences with stress and anxiety. Their stories provide inspiration and a sense of solidarity, reminding you that you are not alone in your struggles.By the end of this chapter, you will have gained a deeper understanding of the importance of mental health and acquired practical strategies for coping with stress and anxiety. You will be equipped with tools to manage stress, build resilience, and prioritize your well-being throughout your college journey and beyond.Remember, mental health matters, and taking proactive steps to care for your emotional well-being is essential. By incorporating the strategies and practices outlined in this chapter, you can cultivate a healthier mindset, develop effective coping mechanisms, and create a supportive environment that promotes mental well-being for yourself and those around you.

Homesickness and Independence; Embracing Change

Leaving the comforts of home and adjusting to a new environment can often evoke feelings of homesickness. In this chapter, we address the challenges of homesickness and the importance of embracing change during your student life journey.We begin by acknowledging that homesickness is a common experience for many students. We explore the emotions associated with homesickness, such as longing for familiar faces, places, and routines. Understanding that these feelings are natural, we provide strategies to help you navigate this transitional phase.One key aspect we delve into is the concept of independence. College is a time when you start to take control of your life and make decisions for yourself. We emphasize the significance of embracing this newfound independence and using it as an opportunity for personal growth.We discuss practical tips for coping with homesickness, such as staying connected with loved ones through technology, seeking support from friends and campus resources, and gradually immersing yourself in campus life. We highlight the importance of engaging in activities that interest you, joining clubs or organizations, and building connections within your new community.Furthermore, we explore the value of creating a home away from home. Whether it's decorating your dorm room with personal touches or finding comfort in familiar hobbies, we provide suggestions for making your living space a welcoming and comforting environment.Additionally, we address the topic of balancing independence and seeking support. While it's important to embrace autonomy, we emphasize the significance of reaching out for help when needed. We discuss the various resources available on campus, such as counseling services, student support centers, and mentors who can provide guidance during times of homesickness.Throughout the chapter, we share personal anecdotes from students who have experienced homesickness and successfully navigated through it. Their stories offer reassurance that homesickness is temporary and can be overcome with time, patience, and a proactive mindset.By the end of this chapter, you will have gained a deeper understanding of homesickness, learned effective strategies for embracing change, and discovered ways to create a sense of belonging in your new environment. Embracing homesickness as a natural part of the transition allows you to fully immerse yourself in the transformative experience of student life while embracing personal growth and independence.

Social Life and Peer Pressure; Making Informed Choices

College is not just about academics; it's also a time for social exploration and building relationships. In this chapter, we delve into the complexities of social life, the influence of peer pressure, and the importance of making informed choices.We begin by emphasizing the significance of finding a healthy balance between socializing and academic responsibilities. We discuss the various social opportunities available on campus, such as clubs, organizations, and events, and provide guidance on how to navigate and manage your social life effectively.Next, we delve into the topic of peer pressure. We explore the different forms of peer pressure that students may encounter, including academic, social, and lifestyle-related pressures. We emphasize the importance of staying true to your values and making choices that align with your personal goals and well-being.Throughout the chapter, we offer practical strategies for making informed decisions and resisting negative peer influences. We discuss the importance of self-awareness, setting boundaries, and developing assertiveness skills. We also address the significance of surrounding yourself with supportive friends who share similar values and goals.Furthermore, we explore the concept of responsible socializing. We provide insights into maintaining a healthy social life while prioritizing your academic success and personal well-being. We discuss strategies for time management, setting priorities, and making conscious decisions about social engagements.Importantly, we touch upon the topic of alcohol and substance use. We provide information on responsible drinking, the potential risks associated with excessive alcohol consumption, and strategies for staying safe in social settings. We emphasize the importance of making responsible choices and seeking help when needed.Throughout the chapter, we incorporate real-life stories and experiences from students who have navigated social life and peer pressure successfully. These stories serve as valuable examples of making informed choices, overcoming challenges, and finding a balance between socializing and personal growth.By the end of this chapter, you will have gained a deeper understanding of the dynamics of social life. in college, developed strategies for resisting negative peer pressure, and learned how to make informed choices that align with your values and goals. This knowledge will empower you to cultivate a fulfilling and positive social experience while maintaining your individuality and well-being.

Career Exploration; Preparing for the Future

As you embark on your student life journey, it's essential to start thinking about your future career path. In this chapter, we explore the importance of career exploration, the benefits of early preparation, and the steps you can take to set yourself up for success.We begin by emphasizing the significance of self-reflection and understanding your interests, values, and skills. We discuss various methods for self-assessment, such as career assessments, personality tests, and exploring your passions. By gaining a deeper understanding of yourself, you'll be better equipped to make informed decisions about your career path.Next, we delve into the exploration of different career options and industries. We provide insights into researching potential careers, gathering information about job prospects, salary expectations, and required qualifications. We encourage you to explore a variety of career paths, keeping an open mind and considering fields that align with your interests and goals.Within this chapter, we also discuss the importance of gaining practical experience through internships, part-time jobs, or volunteer work. We highlight the benefits of these opportunities, including skill development, networking, and exploring potential career paths. We provide guidance on how to secure internships, make the most of these experiences, and leverage them for future career opportunities.Furthermore, we address the value of networking and building professional connections. We discuss strategies for networking, attending career fairs, and leveraging online platforms such as LinkedIn. We emphasize the significance of cultivating relationships with professionals in your field of interest, seeking mentorship, and tapping into the hidden job market.Additionally, we explore the importance of developing transferable skills that are valuable in any career. We discuss skills such as communication, problem-solving, teamwork, and adaptability. We provide guidance on how to develop and showcase these skills to prospective employers.Throughout the chapter, we incorporate practical tips, real-life examples, and success stories of students who have navigated career exploration successfully. Their experiences offer inspiration and guidance as you embark on your own career journey.By the end of this chapter, you will have gained a deeper understanding of the importance of career exploration, developed strategies for self-assessment and researching career options, and learned practical steps to gain relevant experience and build professional connections. This knowledge will empower you to make informed decisions about your career path and lay the foundation for a successful and fulfilling future.

Part-Time Jobs and Internships; Gaining Professional Experience

Obtaining professional experience during your student years can greatly enhance your future career prospects. In this chapter, we delve into the realm of part-time jobs and internships, exploring their significance, benefits, and strategies for securing valuable professional experience.We begin by highlighting the importance of gaining practical experience while studying. We discuss how part-time jobs and internships can provide you with real-world exposure, allowing you to apply theoretical knowledge in a professional setting. We emphasize the value of hands-on experience and its impact on developing transferable skills and expanding your professional network.Next, we delve into the different types of part-time jobs available for students. We discuss various industries and sectors that commonly hire students, such as retail, hospitality, tutoring, or campus positions. We provide insights into the benefits of part-time employment, including financial stability, skill development, and time management skills.Within this chapter, we also explore the world of internships. We discuss the importance of internships in gaining industry-specific experience, building a professional network, and exploring potential career paths. We provide guidance on finding internships, preparing application materials, and interviewing successfully. We also highlight the significance of internships in making informed career decisions and securing future job opportunities.Furthermore, we address the topic of balancing work and academic responsibilities. We provide strategies for effective time management, prioritization, and maintaining a healthy work-life balance. We discuss the importance of open communication with employers, setting realistic expectations, and seeking support when needed.Additionally, we explore the benefits of networking and building connections through part-time jobs and internships. We discuss strategies for professional networking, leveraging relationships with colleagues and supervisors, and utilizing networking platforms such as LinkedIn. We emphasize the long-term value of building a strong professional network and the potential career opportunities that may arise from it.Throughout the chapter, we incorporate real-life examples and success stories of students who have gained valuable professional experience through part-time jobs and internships. These stories serve as inspiration and offer insights into the impact of practical experience on career development.By the end of this chapter, you will have gained a deeper understanding of the significance of part-time jobs and internships, developed strategies for securing valuable professional experience, and learned how to navigate the balance between work and academics. This knowledge will empower you to proactively seek opportunities for professional growth, enhance your resume, and pave the way for a successful career after graduation.

Relationships in College; Love, Friendship, and Boundaries

College is a time of significant personal growth and the formation of lasting relationships. In this chapter, we explore the complexities of relationships in college, including romantic partnerships, friendships, and the importance of setting healthy boundaries.We begin by discussing the significance of self-awareness and personal growth within relationships. We emphasize the importance of understanding oneself, including values, boundaries, and goals, as a foundation for building healthy connections with others. By cultivating self-awareness, you can navigate relationships more effectively and make choices that align with your personal well-being.Next, we delve into the topic of romantic relationships in college. We explore the unique dynamics and challenges that can arise when navigating romantic partnerships while pursuing higher education. We discuss topics such as communication, trust, and compromise, providing strategies for building and maintaining healthy relationships.Within this chapter, we also address the importance of friendships during college. We discuss the role of friendships in providing support, companionship, and a sense of belonging. We explore strategies for building meaningful friendships, navigating conflicts, and maintaining a healthy balance between social life and individual growth.Furthermore, we explore the concept of setting boundaries within relationships. We discuss the significance of establishing clear expectations, communication styles, and personal boundaries to ensure mutual respect and emotional well-being. We provide guidance on assertiveness skills, effective communication techniques, and recognizing when boundaries are being crossed.Additionally, we address the topic of diversity and inclusivity within relationships. We discuss the importance of embracing diversity, cultural differences, and perspectives within your social circle. We encourage open-mindedness, empathy, and respect for others' identities and backgrounds.Throughout the chapter, we incorporate real-life stories and experiences of students who have navigated various types of relationships successfully. These stories serve as examples and provide insights into building healthy connections, navigating challenges, and fostering personal growth through relationships.By the end of this chapter, you will have gained a deeper understanding of relationships in college, developed strategies for fostering healthy romantic partnerships and friendships, and learned how to set and respect personal boundaries. This knowledge will empower you to cultivate meaningful connections, navigate relationship challenges with grace, and create a supportive and inclusive social environment during your college years.

Cultural Diversity; Embracing Differences and Building Connections

In this chapter, we explore the importance of cultural diversity in the college environment and highlight the value of embracing differences while building meaningful connections. We recognize that college campuses are often melting pots of diverse backgrounds, perspectives, and experiences, and understanding and appreciating cultural diversity can enrich your educational journey.

We begin by emphasizing the significance of embracing diversity and fostering an inclusive mindset. We discuss the benefits of engaging with individuals from different cultures, ethnicities, and backgrounds. By actively seeking out opportunities to learn about diverse cultures, attending multicultural events, and participating in intercultural dialogue, you can broaden your horizons and gain a deeper understanding of the world around you.

Next, we delve into the concept of cultural competence, which involves developing the knowledge, skills, and attitudes necessary to interact respectfully and effectively with individuals from diverse backgrounds. We discuss strategies for cultivating cultural sensitivity, including active listening, open-mindedness, and empathy. By embracing cultural diversity and cultivating cultural competence, you can build connections, foster meaningful relationships, and contribute to a more inclusive and harmonious campus community.

Within this chapter, we also explore the challenges and opportunities that arise from cultural diversity. We address topics such as cross-cultural communication, resolving cultural misunderstandings, and navigating potential conflicts. We highlight the importance of respectful dialogue, seeking common ground, and celebrating the richness of diversity. By embracing cultural differences and approaching interactions with an open and curious mindset, you can create bridges of understanding and promote a welcoming and inclusive campus environment.

Personal Growth; Discovering Yourself Outside the Classroom

In this chapter, we shift our focus to personal growth and the importance of discovering oneself outside the academic realm. While college is a time of rigorous study and intellectual development, it is also a transformative period for personal exploration, self-discovery, and self-actualization.

We begin by emphasizing the significance of stepping outside your comfort zone and exploring new experiences. We encourage you to embrace opportunities for personal growth, such as joining clubs and organizations, participating in community service, and taking on leadership roles. These experiences can expand your horizons, challenge your beliefs, and help you discover new passions and interests.

Next, we delve into the concept of self-discovery and reflection. We discuss the importance of self-awareness, introspection, and understanding your values, strengths, and aspirations. By engaging in self-reflection exercises, setting personal goals, and seeking experiences aligned with your authentic self, you can embark on a journey of personal growth and fulfillment.

Within this chapter, we also explore the role of resilience and adaptability in personal growth. We discuss the challenges and setbacks that may arise during your college journey and provide strategies for bouncing back, learning from failures, and developing resilience. We encourage you to embrace a growth mindset, cultivate a positive attitude, and view challenges as opportunities for personal development.

Additionally, we address the significance of building a support network and seeking mentorship. We discuss the benefits of connecting with faculty members, upperclassmen, and alumni who can provide guidance, support, and valuable insights. We also highlight the importance of seeking mentors who can inspire and challenge you, helping you navigate your personal and professional development.

IIealth and Wellness; Prioritizing Self-Care

In this chapter, we emphasize the importance of prioritizing your health and well-being throughout your college journey. We recognize that the demands of student life can be overwhelming, and maintaining physical, mental, and emotional well-being is crucial for academic success and overall happiness.

We begin by discussing the significance of self-care and the various dimensions of wellness. We explore strategies for maintaining a healthy lifestyle, including regular exercise, proper nutrition, and adequate sleep. We also delve into the importance of stress management techniques, such as

mindfulness, meditation, and relaxation practices. By prioritizing self-care and incorporating healthy habits into your daily routine, you can enhance your overall well-being and better cope with the challenges of college life.

Next, we address the importance of mental and emotional well-being. We discuss the impact of stress, anxiety, and other mental health issues on academic performance and personal happiness. We provide resources and strategies for seeking mental health support, such as counseling services, therapy, and support groups. We also emphasize the significance of self-awareness and self-care practices that promote positive mental and emotional health.

Within this chapter, we also explore the importance of creating a balanced and supportive social life. We discuss the benefits of maintaining healthy relationships, setting boundaries, and nurturing connections with friends and loved ones. We encourage you to seek social support, engage in activities that bring you joy, and foster a sense of belonging within your college community.

Additionally, we address the significance of preventive healthcare and maintaining regular check-ups. We provide guidance on accessing healthcare services on campus, understanding insurance coverage, and prioritizing preventive measures such as vaccinations and screenings. By taking proactive steps towards your physical well-being, you can prevent potential health issues and ensure your overall vitality.

Furthermore, we explore the impact of technology and digital well-being on our health. We discuss the importance of managing screen time, practicing digital detox, and maintaining a healthy relationship with technology. By setting boundaries and creating a healthy balance between online and offline activities, you can safeguard your mental and emotional well-being.

Throughout this chapter, we incorporate practical tips, personal anecdotes, and expert advice to guide you in prioritizing your health and well-being. We emphasize that self-care is not selfish but rather a necessary foundation for personal and academic success. By making your health and well-being a priority, you can approach your college journey with vitality, resilience, and a sense of fulfillment.

Remember, by prioritizing self-care and seeking support when needed, you are investing in your long-term well-being. By incorporating the strategies and practices outlined in this chapter, you can create a solid foundation for a healthy and balanced college experience, laying the groundwork for a fulfilling and thriving future.